I0168172

Raising Black Flags

Raising Black Flags:
Original Poetry By and About Pirates

Edited by Stephen Sanders

With the poetry of Flora Alomari, J. L. Bright, Chuck Burrows, Sandra L. Harris, Cassidy King, Shari Land, Shana L. Martin, Michael Muller, Debra Estes Peterson, Melody Sanders, Stephen Sanders, Desiree Simons, Kittye Williams, Pamala A. Williams, and the artwork of Robert L. Berry, Jr., and Kenneth King.

Published by Blackbead Books
www.Blackbead-jewelry.com
ISBN: 978-0-615-25535-4

"The Homecoming of Danny Fry" first appeared in <u>Characters: The Buffalo Soldier and Other Poems</u>, by Stephen Sanders; Lulu.com, 2008.

"Prize Island" first appeared in <u>Characters in Black and White</u>, by Stephen Sanders; Blackbead Books, 2008.

Other poems appearing in this compilation have not been previously published; all are original poetry by the various authors who retain the copyright on their work. For further information regarding the individual authors or to request further copies, contact the editor, Stephen Sanders at blackbeads_tc@yahoo.com.

RAISING BLACK FLAGS Copyright © 2008 by various authors

All rights reserved. Printed in the United States of America. No part of this book or these works may be used or reproduced in any manner whatsoever without written permission of the various authors or their agents except in the case of brief quotations embodied in critical articles and reviews. For further information, contact the editor, Stephen Sanders at blackbeads_tc@yahoo.com.

ISBN: 978-0-615-25535-4

To the pirate in all of us.

In the year 2008, a bold band of brave and hardy souls set sail on a journey born of hope and with the twin goals of glory and gold! These seafaring poets and artists, in honor of the spirit of the group, named their vessel the "Adventure" and set out to make their mark upon the pirate genre and do what they could to inspire their readers with tales full of the legends and lore of buccaneers, privateers, mermaids, sirens, and a life at sea. You are invited to sign articles and become a member of the crew! Enjoy these works and may they bring alive your own visions of the swashbuckling world of the

PIRATE!

Table of Contents

Artwork

Flora Alomari: AKA Taffy Saltwater. She's the Captain of the *Libertine* and Landshark No. 1! Hailing from Houston, Texas, Flora is all-pirate. Her contribution to the book is a personal piece that is a reminiscence of a very special person in her life; she keeps the original of this poem in the cuff of her captain's coat so that she can take it out anytime she chooses to be with him again. It is an honor to sail these pages with her!

Robert L. Berry, Jr.: AKA Sakemaster. Robert Berry is already a recognized and storied artist. His works have been chosen for showing in galleries from Texas to New York. The Cadillac Division of the General Motors Company chose one of his pieces to be the showcase for their "Jazz By the Boulevard Festival" in Fort Worth, Texas. His work can be viewed at www.Jazzmaster.imagekind.com.

J. L. Bright: AKA Cookie Breadfruit. Jerri Bright is an artist, a chef, and the mother of four boys. She hails from Beaumont, TX but used to spend her time cavorting in Hawaii, dallying in France, and trudging through the snow in Germany. Jerri is a literary spirit with an eye for the supernatural and she's chosen an interesting topic for her poem: an old pirate in a tavern telling a young lad about the real world of piracy!

Chuck Burrows: AKA Captain Slippery Jack Beaver. A songwriter and a soldier, a poet and a computer magician, Chuck Burrows has been writing and performing songs since he was a teenager. Thanks to Uncle Sam, his travels have included Iraq, Kuwait, Afghanistan, and most of Europe. He has also served as the GM of Hash House Harrier chapters in South Korea, Texas And Arizona.. If you know what that means . . . "on, on!"

Sandra L Harris: AKA: The Right Reverend One Eye, "Madam" Morrigan "Morgan" Blythe. Sandra currently resides in the Dallas area and she's been pirating since 2002. Sandra has been the vendor coordinator for PyrateCon, see www.pyratecon.com, since its inception in 2007. She's also a founding member of the Brotherhood of the Gulf Pirate reenactment group. She served her country proudly in the US Navy and after that was a police officer in Connecticut. She is also a licensed minister in the Church of Spiritual Humanism. Currently her avocation is programming speech recognition applications for IVR (interactive voice response) computers.

Cassidy King: AKA: Cassadass. Currently living on the island of Galveston, once the home of Jean Lafitte, Cassidy is not only a poet but is also an accomplished seamstress. She has a BA in English and is the mother of Campbell King. Can this be her inspiration for her contribution to the book: a poem about a young boy whose father is a pirate and whose long-suffering mother cares so deeply for her child?

Kenneth King: AKA: Calico Roger Kidd. A graduate of the University of Texas with a degree in Radio, Television, and Film, Ken has spent the better part of his life on the move. An Army brat, he has lived in the United States, the United Kingdom, Germany and Japan and has traveled all over Europe. But it wasn't until he came to Texas in 1994 that his ship finally dropped anchor for good.

Shari Land: AKA Rumba Rue. Shari Land has been writing stories and poetry since she was very young. She is an award-winning costumer and Celtic needlepoint artist. Shari is also a licensed Minister through the Ancient Keltic Church of Tujunga, CA, and has an amazing array of talents: award winning western horse show rider, clown, belly dancer, singing and playing the twelve string guitar, making feather hat pins and jewelry to sell, just to name a few! She has had more than her share of debilitating health problems, but that hasn't stopped her from smiling at the world. Her motto is: "Blessed are those who can laugh at themselves, for they shall never cease to be amused."

Michael Muller: AKA Captain Tito. Michael was born in 1968 in Syracuse, NY, and grew up in Batavia, NY. His interest in all things pirate began while writing folklore projects in both elementary school and the Cub Scouts. As the years passed, his interest in pirates became dormant but never disappeared. Then, in 2003, three things happened that brought his interest back: 1) He visited Seattle and shopped at the "Pirate's Plunder" store. 2) He saw the "Pirates of The Caribbean" movie while in Seattle. 3) He walked directly out of that Seattle movie theatre into the revelry of a Seattle Seafair Pirates parade. With the crowds cheering and the cannon firing, Michael's inner pirate was longing to come out - "Captain Tito" was born!

Shana L. Martin: AKA Kendra the Mermaid, Capt Maevous O'Connell, Fox McShane. Little is known about this woman with many names, except she hails from Largo, Florida, has been writing poetry for thirteen years, and her lower limbs don't work as well as others might. Some say, "That's 'cause she was born of the sea, she was, just like the rest of her kin." Still others claim she was injured by the recoil of a cannon during a great battle at sea. Then there is the truth, which is: "She was just born that way!" Cerebral Palsy to be exact. She uses both a manual chair and a motorized one to get out and about. Does it slow her down? Hardly! She says it makes her the fiercest pirate ever to sail the Seven Seas!

Debra Estes Peterson: AKA Red Bess. Born and raised in west central Minnesota, Deb has been writing poetry since she was 11 years old. During her college years, she became interested in the visual arts, producing and directing several experimental films. But writing has always been her preferred form of self-expression, and her most recent work is a collection of poems entitled "Stems & Pieces". By day, Deb sits in front of a computer in the office of a Twin Cities multi-media company. By night, she sits in front of her home computer, dreaming up adventures for a trio of female pirates in the serial "Anne of the High Seas".

Stephen Sanders: AKA: Blackbead. Like so many people, Steve has been writing poetry since he was in grade school. For a long time, "pirate" was just another mask that he put on from time to time when he wasn't being a Civil War soldier or the general of some great army or an adventuring knight rescuing fair damsels and fighting ugly monsters. But, a few years ago, he learned the lessons which form the basis for "Raising the Black Flag" and decided that a pirate is what he truly wanted to be. He's a founding member of the Brotherhood of the Gulf and his home ports are www.Blackbead-jewelry.com and www.Middlefest.com.

Melody Sanders: AKA Captain Jane Jasper. Born in Texas, moved to Oklahoma, then back to Texas, then all over Texas, Melody is the mother of three, stepmother of three, and has a slew of grandkids, great nieces and nephews and they all call her "Momma Mel." She's been a performer most of her life and has been a producer and director of dinner theater. Now, she's taken a hand at writing. Melody likes to wear the Captain's coat in her family . . . and a flintlock and a skeleton-headed rapier! Don't mess with Momma Mel!

<u>Desiree Simons</u>: AKA Desiree Diamonds. Currently living in a small town northeast of Dallas, Desiree is already a published author; check out her work at www.myspeechpro.com. She is also a college professor, a public speaker, a consultant and the single mother of two teenagers. Desiree doesn't dress up as a pirate all the time like the rest of us but her life encompasses some of the same qualities of the true pirate – real hardship, true romance, and the daily struggle to be free. She is joining Flora, Michael and Shana as one of our more romantic writers - her contribution is a free verse piece about lusty love between a woman and her pirate!

<u>Kittye Williams</u>: AKA Captain Emerald Shaunassey. A native of Vinita, Oklahoma, Kittye is the creator, owner, and manager of The Ladies of the Salty Kiss (see their website at www.theladiesofthesaltykiss.com). Kittye comes from a musical background, having performed in a variety of musical ensembles and vocal choirs throughout her school years. Hooked after attending her first renaissance faire, she became a "professional" actress nine years ago. She enjoys making people laugh and tends to be the troupe's practical joker. When not performing with her troupe, she can be found pursuing the other love of her life, nursing.

<u>Pamala A. Williams</u>: AKA Diamond. Pamala, no relation to Kittye (although they both are members of the Ladies of the Salty Kiss) is a native of Tulsa, Oklahoma. She has been performing on stage since she was four years old, adding Renaissance performer to her repertoire in 2000. Pamala enjoys singing, acting, and general tom-foolery. She's a gifted lady, and can often be found writing her own limericks, songs and poetry which she enjoys performing for anyone who will listen.

Preface

This whole thing got started when I sat down and penned a poem about a pirate. After years of plundering, the pirate's homecoming affects a whole tavern full of everyday people, trodden down by life. For on that night, all of his old friends had "become pirates" and they forget their everyday cares and woes and became "free again." That's what the legend of the pirate is all about really; freedom. The reality was probably quite different but we're not dealing with reality here. We deal in legend.

Later, after a parade through the French Quarter of New Orleans as a part of PyrateCon 2008, it became obvious that these days, instead of a clown, the whole world loves a pirate. Blame it on the movies or on the theme park ride or on Robert Newton, but pirates are a favorite genre and have been forever. And there's no sign of them slowing down as a symbol of freedom, adventure, fun, and, okay, a quick ducat or two!

I decided that an entire book of pirate poetry was called for; my own adventures had introduced me to pirate bards from all over the map. I put out the word that articles were ready to be signed and before you know it, this book was sailing out to sea, headed for your home port!

Now, what can you expect to read here? In the first place, do not come to this book expecting to read the tittering wailings of some lily-faced highbrow who thinks they are a poet but are really nothing more than a sloppy stringer-together of words designed to impress you with their feelings or their intellectual posturing! These poets are real people who write, to steal from Copeland (I AM a pirate after all!), a fanfare for the common man.

Expect to here be entertained with stories of the sea and to be enlightened with peeks into the soul of the buccaneer, the hidden nature of the privateer, and the unspoken "arrrrr" of the pirate. These are poems meant to be read aloud. With rum. And maybe with a few flintlock blasts as punctuation. These are poems meant to be enjoyed; tales to transport you out to sea, walking the quarterdeck of your own ship, in search of whatever treasure you desire! So, hoist that anchor, point your bowsprit to the horizon, and get to it!

Thank You

First and foremost, I want to thank my wife, my captain, the lovely "Jane Jasper." Without her support, her courage in helping me find the right words, and her belief in me, this book would never have become a reality. I also want to give special thanks to Mr. Robert Berry, who showed me through the intricacies of the publishing world (look for his work at www.rberryart.com.)

Of course, I am sincerely grateful for this outstanding group of poets. The sweat and blood, tears and ink that have gone into these creations is there for all to see and, in the end, enjoy. I also want to thank our artists – without the stirring images contributed by these two men this book would be missing something essential to the story of the pirate. This crew has sailed to the ends of imagination and beyond in completing this quest!

And, finally, thank you to Peter Blood, Long John Silver, Jamie Waring, Ben Avery, Calico Jack, Mary and Anne, Billy Bones, Edward Teach, William Kidd, Mal Reynolds, Jack Sparrow, Henry Morgan, Danny Fry, and the millions of other pirates, real and imagined, that laid the foundations for this Great Adventure! Fair winds and a fat galleon to ye all!

"All in a Day's Work"
By Kenneth King, ©2008

THE HOMECOMING OF DANNY FRY

It was a cold, stormy night at the Rose & Crown
But all of me regulars were there;
The village of Tween is a proper English town
And I serve proper English fare.

A soul can live a long, hard life
Without traveling from home too far,
A few snotty brats, taxation and debt
Are fair substitutes for the plague and war.

Sitting in the corner was a proof of me point
It was Tom Johns, our town's overworked tailor.
With a family of four and a poor clientele
He barely stayed ahead of the King's jailer.

Most of his pints he drank for free -
He mended me pants and shirts instead.
I felt sorry for the lad: he couldn't sew his taxes
And he couldn't pay his rent with thread.

There were others in the Crown that night
And all were cut from poor Tom's mold.
Clutching their mugs and staring into space,
They stayed to keep out of the rain and the cold.

I was standing back of me bar, pondering all of me friends,
When there arose a sudden commotion outside;
With a bluster and a curse and a cold wet wind
The front door of me pub burst open wide.

In strode a man in a tricorn' hat
Sporting a long beard and a cutlass at his hip,
Wearing buckets, a sash, and a seaman's coat
He looked like the captain of a pirate ship.

With a twinkle in his eye and a toothy gold smile
He took in me pub and the sad-looking crowd.
Shivering off his jacket then turning to the room,
He bellowed out a greeting clear and loud:

"I've sailed with brigands, black, brown, and white;
I've drunk whole wine kegs dry;
I've taken gold prizes from the Spanish and the French;
And I've cheered as me guns let fly."

"I've sailed 'neath starry, Caribbean skies;
I've rounded the Cape to the Horn;
But after spending half me life at sea
I've returned to the village where I was born."

"Chests of gold and jewels have I
And I have stories from where 'ere I roam,
So come, me hearties, the drinks are on me,
'Cause I've come back to make Tween me home!"

His gaze met a room of glazed-over looks,
These men who life had beat down,
So the pirate strode to the center of the room,
And cast his weather eye all around.

"Well, well, lookee there, it's little Tommy Johns,
I remember ye from when I was a lad.
Remember stealing milk from Squire Hunt's cows?
Right imps we were, but never really bad."

"And look over there! It's me 'ol friend, Pat!
I hear ye left the Army late last year.
I'll bet your mum was glad to have ye home;
Now there's a lady I always held dear."

One by one, he called us all by name
And reminded us we'd known him in days gone by,
And it soon dawned upon us that 'neath that shaggy beard,
Was our old friend and neighbor, Danny Fry.

Rising to their feet, me regulars let out a cheer
And all came forward to shake Danny's hand.
Then he tossed me a pouch of silver and gold
And ordered up a meal both great and grand.

As the cook went off to prepare the feast,
I poured the pub's first round of beer,
Then stoking the fire, Danny began to regale us
With tales of his life as a privateer.

He told us of sacking great cities
As he plundered the enemies of the Crown
And he told us of taking a galleon
After bringing it's mainmast down.

Danny made us feel we were with him
As he talked of a ruby necklace and more
That he took from a willing French lady,
Before putting her safely ashore.

Danny knew how to tell a story
And we would listen again and again
As he told of his grand adventures
And the treasures he shared with his men.

Everyone ate and drank their fill that night,
As we devoured Danny's tales of the sea.
We forgot all about our own petty troubles -
We were happy, we were men again, we were free.

With laughter and smiles and friends arm in arm,
We all stumbled off into the morning light,
But none of us cared as we faced our red-eyed day:
Because of Danny, we'd all become pirates that night!

Stephen Sanders
©2008

My Captain

The Captain took my waist
as we danced the Morris in Dover;
The Captain took my heart
as we danced the Gavotte in Calais;
The Captain took my flower
as we danced the Eternal Dance of Love in Dublin.
The English shot down my Captain
and no more will we mark time.
Now at Execution Dock I'll dance the hempen jig
and thrice the tide will flow o'er me.
And then in Fiddler's Green -
O! I'll dance with my Captain once more.

Flora Alomari
©2008

12

Remembrance

I sit upon the gunwale
    At the twilight of the day
And think about my life that was
    And about my life that may

'Twas glorious, the love I had
    And grieved when it was lost
And as the storm of life did blow
    The ship of me was lost

I think about him often
    When work and time allow
A simple scent, a memory
    I grieve still, even now

But here upon this ship of wood
    I work to reclaim my life
My mates are friends, like family
    They mellow out my strife

The lookout says to look ahead
    The bosun says set sail
The captain says I'm not alone
    As the winds begin to wail

For, though we be a mighty crew
    We each have sorrows of past
And everything must come to an end
    For only the sea will last

Pamala A. Williams, ©2007

The Last Watch

On the Last Watch I stand;
Leaning 'gainst the railing,
The sea stretched out a'fore me.
The ship's company quietly gathered 'round.

On the Last Watch I stand;
Free from the surgeon's hand I be,
Pain nay more wracks my body,
Restful, thankfully, at last I am.

On the Last Watch I stand;
N'r more to land will I go,
N'r more will I drink an' dance
N'r more to see those I adore.

On the Last Watch I stand;
The bell has been rung; its toll drifts out.
The Captain has read from the Good Booke,
My Soul has been shriven, my sins are forgiven.

On the Last Watch I stand;
Surrounded by family, some good and some bad.
With a heave and a ho, their task they begin,
Mates at the ready, work roughened hands, oh so gentle
As they slip me down into my last salty kiss.

On the Last Watch I stood,
I lived my life by my wits and m' blade.
I fought the good fight but died just the same.
Doin' what I chose to do, 'neath the flag so bold,
I died in my place, on the Last Watch I stood.

Kittye Williams
©2008

God Take the King!

Ye ask me why I sail the seas beneath a flag stained black,
Why I risk both life and limb and take the pirate tack?
The answer is an easy one, a song I love to sing,
After years of his bloody taxes, I've come to hate the king!

I bear the marks upon me back of scratches from his cat:
Too many times I've come up short when 'is Majesty passed the hat.
Between his taxes and me debts I were stretched as thin as a blade
And it doesn't change me hate one bit that this bed is one I made.

For a king sits on the throne by grace to lift his subjects up
And not to snatch the bread and meat of which their children sup.
I'd've paid me taxes if I could, I swear to this on High,
But I fear I'm weak, because instead, I heeded me family's cry.

Now taxes are a necessary thing, of that I be quite sure,
If a governed land we want to have these levies we must endure.
But never get behind, me friends, pay all your taxes now
For paying but the portion you can the damned King will not allow.

And once he's got his hooks in ye, yer life is a living hell,
Ye canna' rest a moment 'cause he comes to where ye dwell.
At pike point he collects your pay before it can be spent
On niceties like milk or shoes or even to pay the rent.

Me youngest he died coughin' after a winter without a coat,
Me eldest drowned in a summer storm workin' on a fishin' boat,
Me daughter traded her childhood for pennies to help our plight,
Until one cold, dark evenin', when we lost her to the night.

Me wife, me darlin' Maggie, could'na stand to live like this,
So she drank a dram of poison and waited for Death's cold kiss.
But the poison didn't kill her; it simply stole her sight,
And lost in all this darkness she became a Bedlamite.

Now all me stanchions are overboard, me children, me lovely wife,
So I spends me time in the sweet trade, I live the pirate life.
No more will I pay me taxes with coins a coppery-red,
The only tax I'll pay this king is shot that's made of lead.

But don't ye waste a tear, shipmates, feelin' sorry for the likes of me,
For, in truth, I've come to love this life a'sailin' on the sea.
There's rum, there's women, there's adventure, and sometimes even gold,
And maybe me own ship someday if I live to be that old.

And don't forget, me hearties, death is everywhere at sea.
The life of a seadog is a dodgy one, as I'm sure you'll all agree,
And someday I'll find me doorway among these many harms
And go to spend eternity in me lovin' family's arms.

                          Stephen Sanders
                          ©2008

She . . . He

She
Mermaid
Flowing Hair
Ravishing Tail
Waits for her Pirate
To come in his great ship
When he does they get away
They hold hands and swim together
'Neath the moon to an island
They kiss passionately
Gives her a gold charm
With his warm hands
And strong arms
Captain
He

Michael Muller
©2008

A Pirate's Life For Me"
By Kenneth King, ©2008

The Siren and the Pirate

Your throaty voice does fill my mind,
Its timber and pitch sweet as wine.
It follows me through wake and sleep
Filled with longing enough to make me weep.
Your visage I see afore my eyes
Every line and form a delight divine.
Those haunting eyes so deep and clear,
Are to me worth more than gold so dear.
Your words and music only I do hear,
They fill me with longing so bitterly sweet.
To have you always by my side, so near,
Would be a reward of you I entreat.
But our worlds are not of one,
Separate yet together they be;
For yours it be the sea
While mine is the land.
What a sad unending plight,
To see and hear but n'r to touch
A form so sweet and neatly made
To know at my side you will n'r be.
"I shall come to you, I swear" you whisper sweet,
"By moonlight and by ocean wave."
By moonlight and ocean, I do wait.
Standing, looking out o'r the rail hungry for the sight of you.
"I shall see thee in moonlight bright," I reply,
"I shall look to see thee in the ocean's spray."
Within the moon touched salt spray I you do spy,
Waiting and watching from your rocky perch.
What fierce sea raider, oh wielder of death,
Did e'r find themselves in such a plight?
To find their mind befuddled so by song,
With their heart turned from the fight?

Oh what a fine twist of the Fates this be,
What joy those hags must now be enjoying,
To behold the working of their whims set free,
In the tableau on display for all the world to see.
The fiercely proud sea rover, this scoundrel of the seas
Whose hard heart was brought to sway,
The handsome siren, this legend of the briny deep,
Who would give up the sea to live upon the shore.
Fate ensnared them both, this child of land and child of sea,
From separate walks of life they came,
                        the stuff of legends ever more
For who could have foreseen the Siren and his Pirate Queen?

                    Kittye Williams
                    ©2008

Ode to Rumba Rue

She's a rabble rouser, a pirate for sure,
She'll take whatever she can,
And yet she's sweet and so demure,
But always in command.

It's said she steals the night away,
A pickpocket, a sly and wry gal,
From those who are looking the other way,
It doesn't matter in what locale.

It's said she's a descendant of the Killigrew clan
Of royal blood but secretly born,
She quietly treads the common lands
A woman homeless, a woman scorned.

But yet she prevails on ships that sail,
Dressed like a man she hides herself,
She drinks with hardy mug and ale,
Certainly not a doll on a dusty shelf!

But when she's free and feeling the wind,
The ocean breeze and waves that crash,
She'll turn a trick of deadly sins,
The men tumble in piles of wicked abash.

She's no stranger to the pirates she knows,
They respect her prowess and knifely ends,
For not to become one of her deadly throws
They are better off being her friends.

So here's to you, Rumba Rue!
Follow your heart and soul of prizes,
Sail your ship in waters blue,
You're a rabble rouser, through and through!

Shari Land
©2008

The Middle Watch

The loneliest time in the life of a ship:
'Tween the last glimpse of the light of day
And the first rays of the rising sun.
When the stars remind ye how small ye be
And the moon watches yer every move;
Or the night be so black that ye lose yer way
Finding the back of yer hand.
Scanning that horizon of tarry blackness
Even a ship of solid gold would be missed.
But every salt must take a turn
Standing the Middle Watch from time to time.
And it can be a good time for a sailor to think;
Quiet, and steady, and without many surprises
When the water's deep and the map empty.
With no hope of a prize or plunder
The eye can turn inward in search of treasure.
Ye can find yerself in coiling a rope,
Or trimming a sail to a perfect pitch,
Or holding a true course by lamplight
During the alone-est time in a life at sea.

Stephen Sanders
©2008

Note: The "middle watch" runs from midnight to four a.m.

24

La Media Guardia

Los momentos mas solitarios en la vida de un barco:
Entre el último destello de luz del día,
Y los primeros rayos del sol al amanecer.
Cuando las estrellas te recuerdan cuan pequeño eres
Y la luna observa cada movimiento;
O cuando en la noche tan oscura pierdes el camino
Econtrando solo la palma de tu mano.
Divisando el horizonte tan oscuro
Hasta un barco de oro sólido pasaría desapersivido.
Pero cada grano de sal debe tomar el turno
Parado en la media guardia de vez en cuando.
Es un buen momento para un marinero pensar;
En silencio, quieto, y sin sorpresa alguna
Cuando el agua es profunda y el mapa está vacío.
Con ninguna esperanza de premio o contrabando
El ojo puede internalizarse en busca de un tesoro.
Te puedes encontrar enredado en una soga,
O cuidadosamente navegando a un curso perfecto,
O manteniendo el rumbo con la luz de una linterna
Durante los momentos más solitarios en la vida en alta mar.

Translation by Yanira Colon-Torres
©2008

Springs and Neaps

Me mum she does the washin',
Me mum she does the chores,
But me pap he rides the ocean,
Me pap is tougher than yours!

Me mum she does the cookin'
Me mum she keeps me fed.
But me pap's a grand adventurer:
Me pap could shoot yours dead!

Each day he tames the ocean,
Each day he lives his last,
He swings a blade and wields a gun
Across the sea so vast.

Me pap's a gentleman of fortune,
Or so he's fashioned by me mum,
He razes ships and steals their cargo
Of gold and guns and rum.

Mum seems not to think too kindly
Of me pap who raids the sea
She curses him behind her hand
When she thinks that I can't see.

At night she weeps a silent lament
For the man who left her alone
And prays each night in her pious voice
For God to bring him safe home.

Me da' he seems not to think too kindly
Of me mum's weeping prayer,
He only stops in when his big ship is laden
With piles of ill-gotten fair.

Me mum she is a great mystery,
Me mum she makes me wonder:
"Why curse a man and wish him safe?"
It's a thing to sit and ponder.

But then I get to thinkin'
About me pap so brave,
So me mum she slips right out me mind,
And about me pap I rave.

I sometimes think it hurts her,
When I tell her my dream's to join
Me pap aboard his pirate ship
And help him lift some coin.

Once he came to visit us,
To see his "hardy spawn"
And the "wench" what gave him me
But soon again he was gone.

But when in port he told me,
"Son, when a man you finally be,
I'll sail back in and pack you up,
And take you out with me."

"We'll sail the rowdy ocean,
We'll see the sights there be to see
We'll drink rum in foreign ports,
Together you and me!"

And so I swing me wooden sword,
And learn the rules of the sea,
And pretend I'm standing on the deck:
Me pap, the pirate captain, and me.

Cassidy King
©2008

"Castaways"
By Kenneth King, ©2008

Dark Prince of Plunder
Inspired by Captain Siren of the *Poseidon*

I.

He moves silently, like the wind on a moonless night.
Wine, women, and song taken freely, that is his delight.
Eyes that mesmerize, dark as coal,
Gazing too deeply can steal one's soul.
Skin full of warmth and tan,
Liken to the tropics and Jamaican sand
Women adore him, for his velvet smile.
Men scorn him, for leaving them breathless mile upon mile.

II.

No one knows his name,
For deception is his game.
He plays them all like a pipe's song
Then just as quickly he sails on.
He has broken many a heart, both young and old
He is not one to have or to hold.
For his one and only love is me:
The wide vast expanse of the sea.

III.

"Oh daughters of Poseidon, pearls of the ocean
I offer myself to thee in deepest devotion!
All I do ask in return
You give me safe sojourn.
Calm wave and tide
With your sweet song of lullaby."

IV.

"These words you speak are unknown of."
"They are more than words, they are love."
"You give your life to the sea?"
"I give my life, only to thee."
"You are mine O' Dark Prince of Plunder,
And I shall have you and no other!"

Shana L. Martin
©2004

The Captain's Coat

"Get aloft," the captain shouted,
"There's a prize to be taken out there!
Man your guns and prepare for a battle
Each survivor takes an equal share!"

I was sailing on the brig *Adventure*,
A nimbler square-rigger I've never seen
She was stiff, she was yar, she was weatherly,
And her lines were true and clean.

Her captain was a man named Griffin
Who was always ready for a fight
His hand was iron in discipline
But he treated us seadogs right.

He wore a long green gentleman's coat
With a high collar and trim of gold
You could find him on deck with barely a glance
'Cause he always wore it, whether hot or cold.

We bore down on the ship he had sighted
And the crew all gasped in surprise
For there before us, rising up out of the haze,
A Spanish galleon appeared before our eyes.

Tall as a mountain, three times our height,
And that was with her riding low,
And her sides were covered with gun ports:
Twelve on top and twelve below.

I was berthed as Griffin's Master Gunner
And I knew what that broadside could mean
If the Dons knew how to use them
Their guns would sweep our deck clean.

Captain Griffin had always been a brawler
I knew what he intended to do
We'd run in and throw over our grappling hooks
And our boarders would o'erwhelm the crew.

Standing at me station, I trembled,
The sweat was a'crawling down me back.
The 'Venture was running ahead of the wind
Approaching the Dons on their portside tack.

Our decks were cleared for action,
Coming up on the galleon fast,
When I saw the Spaniard turning –
We would suffer at least one blast!

As the big ship turned toward us
I could see we'd slip side by side
And just before we met her
"Get down," the captain cried!

The rest of us dashed for cover,
The battle had truly begun,
We were less than a cable from her
And she let loose with every gun.

Two dozen iron black killers
Came flying at us through the air
And after the bone crushing impacts
There was blood and death everywhere

As we cleared her and the screams got started
I looked around me to measure the cost
The masts were still standing upright
But half of our port cannon were lost.

The men were quick to take stations
Some were wounded but fewer were dead
Unless hit by a ball or flying wreckage
A sailor's wounds were caused by splinters instead.

I ran in search of the captain
And found him to be one of our dead
His body lay limp as a rag doll
His green coat was covered with red

I knew that we should go running
I knew we were outgunned and outmanned
But I knew when I saw the captain's body
That caution and reason were damned

The crew had seen the poor captain
And silence ruled over the boat
But the weary survivors all watched me with awe
As I put on the bloody captain's coat.

"Take heart, ye seadogs, and hear me,
This battle is not over yet,
Listen up and we'll give these poxy Spaniards
A fight they'll never forget!"

"Trim your sails and blow on your matches,
Prepare to cut across her wake
We have the wind in our favor and
We'll give her stern a rake!"

A cheer went up from the crewmen
As I tried to give orders of a sort,
"Man the portside guns you seahawks
And helmsman, HARD A'PORT!"

The nimble *'Venture* swung 'round smartly
And we heeled with hardly a sway
And there sat the Spanish galleon
Resting barely two cables away.

For when she had turned to meet us
In the irons she became firmly locked
With the wind a'blowin' on her bowsprit
She sat as still as if she was docked

But the *Adventure* was like a seabird
Flying light and fast and spry
And even with the wind against us
We were sailing full and by.

Our first broadside was a weak one:
The portside guns were down to five,
But when we came 'round a'tacking,
The starboard guns came alive.

We slowly tacked towards the transom,
Firing each time the guns came to bear,
Turning the *Adventure* as close to the wind
As I could bring myself to dare.

To be sure the stern is a small target,
No matter the ship's great size,
But each hit does maximum damage,
Each hit brings you closer to the prize.

The Spaniard was wallowing windless,
He was trying to turn her in vain,
But the fight went out of him fully
When we parted his iron rudder chain.

At last the galleon struck her colors,
And we boarded her without a fight,
And when we searched out her treasure,
My eyes had never beheld such a sight!

There was a chest flowing over with jewelry:
Emeralds and pearls and more!
There was a bag of gold minted coinage
And silver bars wrought by the score!

We knew that we were all rich men,
At least for a month or two,
And I hoped that we had a bright future:
This was now my ship and my crew.

In addition to the gold, jewels and silver,
The hold was full of gentlemen's dress.
There were silks and brocades a'plenty
And I was tempted I must confess.

But I knew as we made ready to leave her,
As we lowered the treasure to our boat,
That no other jacket would ever fit me
And I still wear Captain Griffin's green coat.

Stephen Sanders
©2008

Steal From Me Tonight

The dark water rhythmically rocks the ship
as I stand against the railing.
Once again, I watch you row
silently into the night.
Moving swiftly toward
the unsuspecting prey.

Soon you will take what is theirs
and make it your own.
But later…much later tonight
you will steal from me.

The longing in your eyes
always conquers my will.
My only option is surrender.
Your touch steals my breath
and your kisses rob me
of all sense of time and place.

There is only you.
My pirate, the keeper of my heart.
Come steal from me tonight

Desiree Simons
©2008

Sailor's Praise

I sit upon the railing of the ship that I call home
And watch the dolphins playfully go swimming in the foam
The creaking of the rigging and the snapping of the sails
The breeze that sends us on our way will cure us of our ails

The moonlight dancing on the waves, the clouds that scuttle by
The songs of giant humpback whales, the stars up in the sky
The gentle sway of hammocks in our quarters as we sleep
The dark blue of the ocean that reminds us that it's deep

The albatross that settles in the rigging for a rest
Proves that of all long-distant birds this gooney is the best
The salt sea spray kisses my face as I stand upon the bow
And I wonder what would have happened if I wasn't here,
        if this wasn't now

To never see the ocean, the glimmer of the sea?
To never sail upon a ship, oh that could not be me
To live my life upon the land as dry as dry could be?
Praise be, 'tis but a nightmare, I'm where I'm supposed to be

Pamala A. Williams
©2008

So Ye Want To Be A Pirate

 So ye want to be a pirate,
And sail the seven seas,
Taking ships with chests of gold
And bringing admirals to their knees!

Well, when I was young, I thought the same,
And look at where it's brought me:
Not one piece of gold, not one fancy bead,
Just this splintered stick where me leg ought to be!

Come sit at me table and I'll pour ye some ales
And fill yer head up with the Devil's own tales!
Of ships black as midnight and monsters with eyes that glow,
More horrible things than any young lad should know!

Me head be full of memories: of wooden ships and iron men,
Of the restless wind and the endless sea.
I went sailin' for treasure and fightin' for me life
With not a single true friend beside me.

Back then I thought I was smart as a whip!
I drank with some pirates and worked on their ship.
I tried to be just like one of the crew
'Til the day I found myself tight in their grip.

I started out as a cabin boy, as low as I could be,
But a'fore long I worked meself up to ship's cook . . .
Oh, lad! The things I have seen! The things I have done!
They'd fill up a spine-tingling book!

I saw brave men made to walk the plank,
With sharks a'waitin' most didn't swim but a few feet:
They screamed, "God help me" as they were pulled under
And the sea ran as red as a beet.

I been shot and I been stabbed
A dozen times or more;
I shook hands with ol'Davy Jones
And sailed too near to Fiddler Green's shore.

I once had a lass as pretty as she could be!
Her eyes were filled with love and a heart that was true;
She waited and waited till she could wait no more
And married the old man that owned the barrel store.

I'm telling ye lad it's not a great life,
I'd give it all to have that lass for me wife!
I have nothing to show for me years climbin' sails
But a few curly scars and these bloody pirate tales!

I remember the day we took the Sea Pearl,
Her captain were named Shark Tooth Bill,
Bill stood on the deck with sword in his hand
He was ready to maim and ready to kill!

We fought day and night for most of three days;
Buccaneers fell left and right!
Then on the fourth day, no noise was heard;
But, oh, lad, it was a terrible sight!

Bill, he were the last to go, he held on to the end,
He cried out, "I'll be back, all you 'lubbers'll see!"
A'fore he moved to the rail, he rang the ships bell,
And then he jumped overboard, down into the sea!

On some nights, when the thick fog rolls in,
If ye listen, ye will hear that ship's bell!
Then beware, me lad, for out of the mist
Bill's ship will come sailin' straight from Hell!

Ye'll see a strange light, as the ghost ship appears,
And too late it'll be to run and hide,
There'll be ol'Bill, standing tall against the wind,
He'll be comin' for ye to sail by his side!

On that ship, forever ye'll stand watch,
The cold wind and rain in your hair.
Ol'Bill will be laughing and call ye by name
For he knows ye will always be there.

It's a sad life I've led, one I'd not do again,
Sailing under "jolly rogers" both black and red.
I hope ye've listened and learned my hard lesson:
If you have, ye'll stay home in your bed

J.L. Bright
©2008

Pirate Prince's Vow
Inspired By: God and Siren (AKA Kim)

I.

I have sailed the seven, searching for that small bit o' heaven
Since the age of three, nothing compares to she.
I've watched her walk the moon kissed surf
And give silent praise to the one who gave her birth.
As the waves did roll, into the water she did stroll
With long raven hair covering just so, all that God gave her
        would just barely show.
Then something caught me by surprise, when I saw her limbs and thighs
Transform themselves into a sailor's deepest wish -
        that of a tail of the largest fish!
Green as the color of the seas, the sight of this made me weak in the
knees.
She swayed her way through the wake,
My heart pounded so I thought it would break.
I saw the green with gold fleck in her eye, as she came close I was
petrified.
When she spoke it was like an angelic choir igniting my very desire

II.

"Oh brave prince of pirates who pillage and plunder,
Like a child, you shake and shudder.
Your adventures and exploits are legendary, always sailing
        to places dark and scary,
Ready to give the largest galleon a good race,
Yet like a rabbit your heart beats at a quicker pace.
By your scars and wounds I surmise, many a man has met their demise.
Nothing seems to phase you, not even in battle,
So, tell me what has you in such a rattle?
You once proclaimed your only love was the sea, and in so saying
        you also love me!
Remember always as now, your precious promise and sacred vow!"

42

III.

In the early light of dawn, I found that she was gone.
Was it real as it did seem, or was it all just an elaborate dream?
The image of her is still etched in my memory for all of eternity
The saltiness of her kiss fills me with an intoxicating bliss!
I search the seas in vain, hoping to catch just a glimpse of her again.
O' maiden of the sea, wherefore do you hide from me?

IV.

"What such a man is this, pirate prince
That women should faint for a simple kiss?"
His arrogance can be seen a fathom away simply by the way
       he talks and sways!
See how easily they take to his arm, as he weaves his not so subtle charm.
They blush giggle and sigh, unaware of the glint in his eye.
"What be your scheme?" I glare, "of your kind I am fully aware!"
He stopped short on deck, he glared back and grabbed my neck.
But I showed no fear, as he bent close to my ear,
"You have spirit and flame, I like a woman who knows the rules
       of the game!"
Boiling, my fury I wanted him to taste, so with all in me I slapped his
face!
Unmoved he rubbed his chin and asked, "Care to go again?"
But before I could deliver another blow, I was over his shoulder
       and off we did go.

V.

Like a great water spout, she fussed, fretted, twirling about.
Yelling and ranting at the top of her lungs, I waited patiently
       till she was done!
"Are you quite finished now?" I said, that was when she walloped my
head.
Then she cackled with glee,
"Serves you right for what you have done to such as me!"

I decided then this was of no use, so I put out my hand and called it truce.
It was at that moment I did realize that I was staring into
        those same green eyes!
"Wherefore do you look at me so? Release my hand, let it go!"
"I can not let you back to sea, where my heart is,
        that is where you should be."
"What are these words you say is this part of the game you play?
For I have known many like you who break hearts before they
are through."
"The words I speak are foreign even unto me,
        but you have set this captive free."

VI.

He is most unwell, certainly under my most powerful spell!
 There was something in his words that rang so true,
        I knew at once what I must do.
I prayed for the moon to rise, for I must go back into the sea,
And undo the bonds that behold him to me.
"Do you not love me? Why must you go?"
"I love you more than you could ever know. . .
Remember always as now, your precious promise and sacred vow!"

Shana L. Martin
©2007

The Ocean's Prize

The boards creaked,
Straining loudly,
Splintering.
Fragments, like missiles of fiery steel,
Rained down upon the sea.

Voices of men cried out
As the Ocean swallowed its prize.

Barely a sound as all becomes quiet,
The fingers of the Ocean have grasped another ship
To lie down upon the deep bed of sand,
Never again to see dry land.

Shari Land
©2008

45

The Turncoat

I went to sea to defend my country.
I went to sea to see the wide world.
I went to sea to learn a new trade.
I went to sea to support my family.

I stayed at sea because my country needed me.
I stayed at sea to repel the world.
I stayed at sea to ply my new trade.
I stayed at sea to honor my family.

I left behind the bloody King's Navy.
I left behind the cruel world I knew.
I left behind my old mop and my sometimes pay.
I left behind my family so far away.

I learned a new life and joined a new "navy."
I learned a new world full of death and uncertainty.
I learned a new trade, so bold and daring.
I learned of my family's despair and shame.

I was caught after three years of mayhem.
I was repelled by the world I had once repelled.
I was stripped of my trade, my skill all for naught.
I was despised and denounced by my kith and kin.

I was hung by the damned King's Navy.
I was paraded before the world for all to see.
I was stripped of m' skills, m' trade, and m' life.
I was abandoned, left to rot by my family.

I was once a sailor who proudly went to sea.
I was once a doe-eyed lass out to see the world.
I was once a skill-less wanderer with no future.
I was once a beloved daughter, a sister, an aunt.

I am no more but a memory across the endless sea.
I am no more to the world save a myth to be scoffed at.
I am no more, my skills long faded into mists.
I am no more but a ghost to my family, a shadow fastly fading.

I am the ghost of pirates past.
I am the stuff of legends vast.
I am the dream of lasses still.
I am the hope of all who will.

Kittye Williams
©2008

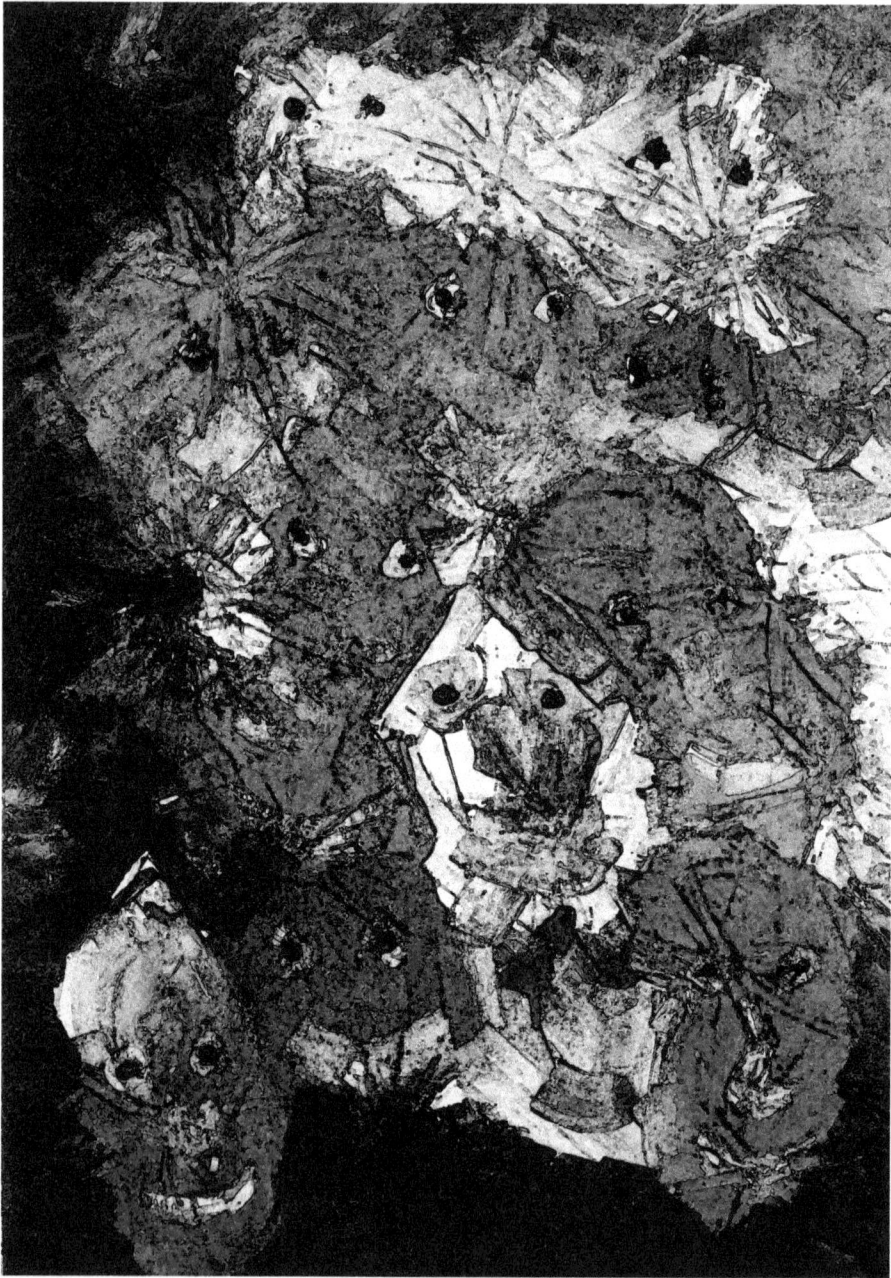

"Ghost Pirates"
By Robert L. Berry, Jr., ©2008

The Ghost Pirates

Ghost Pirates
They Roam the Seas
Searching for Pleasures
Hoping for Treasures
Ghost Pirates
Thieves of the Sea
Ghost Pirates
Bandits of the Ocean
Striking Fear with Emotion
Causing Untold Commotion
Ghost Pirates
Bandits of the Ocean

Robert L Berry Jr.
©2008

A Tale From The Devil's Tavern

Gather around me, ye brave seadogs,
And I'll tell ye a tale of the sea,
Believe what ye will when I'm finished,
But remember that no tale is free.

Twenty years ago I was a pirate,
Aboard the *Sabre*, a swift, deadly ship.
We were out of Port Royal, Jamaica,
Raidin' the Main on that particular trip.

I was hard at work in the galley,
Cuttin' bits from a big bacon slab,
When I heard the older men talkin',
And I caught a bit of their gab . . .

"By gar, ye all be superstitious,
I care not what any of ye say,
I see yer crosses and amulets and medallions
And yer wren's feathers from last New Year's Day."

"Ye all believe in ghoulies and ghosties,
And things that rise out of the sea,
And many of ye call on St. Elmo,
Oh, aye, ye canna' fool me!"

"I heard the stories a'fore I signed articles,
And even more I've endured since then,
I know ye've heard it yourselves at least once
But listen up and I'll tell ye again."

"There's a ghost who visits the *Sabre*,
And tho' she only comes one night a year,
She never leaves alone in the mornin'
And where she goes is a place we all fear."

"She walks the deck at midnight,
Flamin' hair and a gown of mist,
Her face a mask of fiery rage,
Her hand an icy fist."

"In life she was a lovely senorita,
Taken from a town on the Main;
Beaten and abused by a savage pirate crew,
Her torturers finally drove her insane."

"They kept her in chains below deck,
With little or nothing to eat.
It was only after the worst was all over
That they found the ship's rats were her meat."

"One night a scalawag came to take her,
Like a fool he let loose her chains.
And swingin' 'em like a scythe blade,
She decorated the bulkhead with his brains."

"Screamin' then like a banshee,
She ran out onto the deck,
Startlin' the first pirate she came to,
She turned his face into a mangled, bloody wreck."

"Her screams brought the watch to attention,
And they soon cornered the little Spanish tart,
And with a fine shot from his flintlock,
The captain put a ball in her heart."

"If they'd pitched her into the sea it'd been over,
But they bound her and pulled her up with a jerk,
And hung her from the bunt on the mainmast
To let the seagulls and petrels do their work."

"Now seabirds be right hungry fellows,
I can't stand their shrill, screechin', cries,
And we all know that when they start eatin' ,
They begin with the lips and the eyes."

"She hung there through both the dog watches,
And the helm said he glimpsed her that night,
But when the sun rose over the horizon,
The little lady was nowhere in sight."

"They say they never found her body,
Not a rag or a thread from her gown,
Some say she drifted up to Heaven,
But I think a squeamish crewman cut her down."

"But in yer stories she comes back for vengeance,
Takin' a crewman on the anniversary of that night,
And without any screams or blood or noise,
She drags them off into the silvery moonlight."

"And tonight's the very night ye all tell me,
And it's the midnight watch that I've drawn,
I suppose that ye expect me to be cowerin'
And prayin' to God that I see dawn."

"Well, ye won't catch me singin' 'hallelujah,'
Or wearin' a magic geegaw someplace,
Just look for me in the mornin'
And I'll be laughin' right to yer face!"

He smirked as he rose from the table,
Leavin' behind a dozen other men,
Who judgin' by the looks on their faces,
Believed that they'd never see him again.

I vowed to spend that night above deck,
Being young, I wanted to see what I could see,
But mornin' found me asleep on the hawser,
And the ship was as quiet as can be.

The men were noticeably silent,
They had been that way since dawn,
For when the mornin' watch had taken over
The laughin' unbeliever was gone.

Of him we found neither hide nor hair,
But in truth it wasn't much of a loss;
The sea deals harsh to a man without faith
And I think I'll just keep wearin' me cross.

I pray that it keeps me safe on the ocean,
Or if not, that it leads me to the light,
For at dusk I board the *Sabre* again:
And I stand the midnight watch tonight.

She walks the deck at midnight,
Flaming hair and a gown of mist,
Her face a mask of fiery rage,
Her hand an icy fist.

Stephen Sanders
©2008

<u>Pirates!</u>

*P*lunderers of the oceans, dressed
*I*n
*R*iches and in rags.
*A*vid, a-r-r-dent
*T*reasure-Seekers.
*E*nthusiastic
*S*calawags!

Melody Sanders
©2008

The Only Way

As I walked out onto the deck in the morning,
The bodies of those who died in glory,
Wrapped in canvas and tied with rope,
They laid there like pillars of stone with no hope.

They fought like the devils we knew them to be,
The fiercest of pirates they were told to me,
They sailed the sea of treasures untold,
They fought like heroes, true and bold.

I would watch them from the rigging above,
Mastering their skills with care and love:
One was an artist of fine wood carvings,
Another sewed the sails with distinctive markings.

But the youngest, a lad barely of ten,
A fine powder monkey he was and a friend,
To whom many gave him tidbits of goods,
To which he crafted into small boats of wood.

But now they lay, three bodies slayed,
They had fought gallantly to the end they say,
How sad to lose their lives upon the sea
But that was the life of a pirate's spree.

As I watch the bodies slide into the sea,
And sink in the dark waters, their souls now free,
Through stormy seas and fine clear days,
'Tis a pirate's life and their life their way.

Shari Land
©2008

Farewell, Brave Lion

I took you from a Spanish captain,
Back in seventeen-oh-two,
I knew it was your maiden voyage:
Your sails were still brand new.

You handled like an Irish racehorse,
Headstrong but steady and true,
And with the slightest breezes
There was nothing I couldn't ask of you.

You managed fourteen cannon
Without giving up a knot
And in every fight but the last one
You gave better than you got.

It was my mistake to fight a carrack
With a twenty-four gun array
And now you lie forever
'Neath the blue of Santiago Bay.

It's been years since first I boarded you,
Now your sailing days are through,
Your guns have all gone silent:
I finally asked too much of you.

Stephen Sanders
©2008

The Adventurer (Jonathan Hawks)

He cut a dashing figure on deck
Resembling a dagger to the neck.
Misty gray-blue, his glare
Only the sea can compare.
Hair, dark and soft as raven's wing
This, self proclaimed, "Pirate King!"

"Jonathan Hawks belongs in the stocks
Jonathan Hawks will lose more than his locks!"

He sails not for fame or lady's pleasure
He is purely an adventurer.
Seeking that which was lost,
No matter what the cost.
Life or limb
Is all the same to him.

"Jonathan Hawks belongs in the stocks
Jonathan Hawks will lose more than his locks!"

Shana L. Martin
©2005

The Golden Age of Piracy

I sat upon the bench and gazed out to sea,
And pondered over my thoughts that carried me to dream.
My weathered and wrinkled hands, tanned deeply by the sun,
Bore signs of past wounds and my fingers curled by tendons undone.

Those were the days, when I was young and lithe
A pirate by choice and a fighter by night.
I had sailed the Caribbean taking prizes of silks and spices
But it twas the rum that kept me in many drunken vices.

I laughed to myself at the ridiculous stories,
That pirates walked their captors across a plank of bloodied glory,
Or that they buried their treasures into the ground,
Why do that when treasures were meant to be found?

A pirate's life was no life of glory,
A bloody savage world in the ocean waters of a story,
Ragged and diseased as many were,
How did the rumors become to be so blurred?

Perhaps I will never know the paths that led through the age,
But my time has come to an end and I'm old with breakage,
But through my old and feeble eyes of unwritten literacy,
I was part of the Golden Age of Piracy.

Shari Land
©2008

The Captain and The Mermaid

I

The Captain Sets sail.
He searches for his treasure.
He spys a mermaid.

She waves right to him.
She is a beautiful one.
He dives to meet her.

They swim together.
The Captain kisses her hand.
She kisses him back.

The mermaid leads him
to where his treasure is found.
He tries to take it.

The waves get restless.
She leads him back to his ship.
She has saved his life.

His treasure is her.
Not gold or silver doubloons.
He loves her always.

II

A Captain's Longing

A pyrate captain sails the sea.
A lovely mermaid he doth spy.
With her he doth wish to be.
Or that he would rather die.

So to her side he did flee.
Her lovely name he did cry.
Their hearts did beat so rapidly
For a love that neither could deny.

III

There she dreams of him,
in the warm and still Lagoon,
waiting for his ship.

He sails in close by,
sees her from the quarter deck,
in the still moonlight.

The Captain cries out
to the lovely mermaid lass,
"Will she come aboard?"

Her heart is racing.
She has dreamt of being held
in his arms so strong.

He kisses her deep,
on her lips so ruby red,
making her so hot.

With his hook he strokes,
up and down her golden hair,
giving her the chills.

She feels his muscles,
with her hands so soft and smooth.
He breaths deep and slow.

They dive off the deck,
and swim to her lair below,
to make wild romance.

They love each other.
The Captain and the mermaid,
are a couple now.

IV

<u>My Dearest Pirate</u>

My dearest Pirate
I want to be your lover
by your side on board.

My dearest Pirate
I wish to be your mermaid,
to guide you safely.

My dearest Pirate
I wish for you to hold me
and stroke my long tail.

My dearest Pirate
I dream of you each evening
in the still moonlight.

V

The stormy winds blew
It made the mermaid feel sad
Her Captain's ship lost

The rain was quite strong
The waves were out of control
She had lost her love

At last it all broke
The storm was moving away
The winds were dying

The sun it did show
She could see her love again
It made her feel warm

His ship made it through
The mermaid swam out to him
They were together

VI

The Captain and His Maid

The beautiful mermaid comes to the surface.
Her gorgeous shadow reflects on the tide.
She takes a deep breath of the fresh sea air.
Waiting for her captain to sail on by.
She waits with each wave
and with each gentle breeze.
She waits.
She waits
with a tear in her eye.

The handsome Captain is on the main deck.
He stands like a trophy leading his crew.
He looks through his scope out on the horizon
hoping to see his mermaid love.
He looks at the small waves down below.
He looks.
He looks
at the large waves above.

The maid and captain spy each other.
Their hearts are beating and their spirits both rise.
He dives overboard and swims quickly toward her
wanting to hold the desire of his life.
They kiss as they meet.
Their lips well connected.
They kiss.
They kiss
like a new man and wife.

Michael Muller, ©2008

The Angel of Death

Her merry laughter fills the pub
Where the sailors gather
They buy her rum and crowd around
Her affection they are after

A siren from the ocean deep
Her beauty is enthralling
She smiles and listens with intent
To tales they are recalling

A handsome pirate steals her eye
A heavy purse he carries
With gold and silver he makes to woo
But his actions make her wary

"Alas, m'lord, I'm not a wench.
You cannot buy my kisses.
I, too, a skull and crossbones fly.
None stand against my wishes."

He draws his blade, but much too slow
Her loveliness, it blinds him
The sorceress, her deadly spell
Has captured him and binds him

The woman with the blackened heart
Offers up her best:
A cutlass swept across his throat
A dagger in his chest

She leaves a kiss upon his lips
A wine-sweet taste that thrills him
Yet as she spills the pirate's blood
'Tis a broken heart that kills him

Debra Estes Peterson
©2008

Rana

A crowded, smoke-filled jungle clearing:
Pulsing drums, gyrating bodies,
A swirl of raucous pleasure.

So exotic and new to me
And yet as old as the world.

And then you are there,
Shouting your name so I can hear it:
"Ranavalona, but they call me Rana."
Half French and half Merinha, you say,
You tell me you are "Hova" but to me it sounds like "home,"
Your smile, your laughter,
The sparkle of the firelight in your eyes . . .

And then we slip away into the night
To share a dance all alone.
Your face framed in my hands . . .
Your whispered words in pidgin French
Become a song in my ear . . .
The movement of your body under my hand . . .

Then, later, I lean close, to give you a gift of pearls
Taken from a treasure chest aboard a Moghul galleon
Bound for Persia from the Indee.
Even now, years later,
I feel the warmth and the weight
Of your breast against my chest.

A moment of intimacy in a river of time
But it marks itself as a memory
On a day that I can never forget.
Enchanté, mademoiselle, enchanté, Rana.

Stephen Sanders
©2008

A Sailor's Life For Me

Tis a sailor's life for me, ohhh off to high ole sea!
With my rucksack o'r my shoulder
And m' feet all clattering down
Tis a sailor's life for me, ohhh off to the high ole sea!

Oh, tis you an' me an the Skipper to boot,
Wc're off to the high seas, lookin' for loot.
We're not coming home for many a month,
Tis a sailor's life for me, ohhh off to the high ole sea!

There's sails to be trimmed and rigs to be set
        and the bilges they need a'pumping,
There's fish to be caught and decks to be scrubbed
        and still those bilges need pumping.
There's rum to be drunk and jigs to be danced
        and by God, those bilges need dumping.
Tis a sailor's life for me, ohhh off to the high ole sea!

The Skipper got pissed and the Mate is crazy
        and the Cook's pulling double duty,
The Bosun be mad and the Carpenter's been nailed
        and the Monkeys are all fruity.
The Cabin Boy got sloshed and the crew's all
        blue-blooded paralytic drunk but,
Tis a sailor's life for me, ohhh off to the high ole sea!

Twelve months have come and gone since we left port,
The trip's been long and the weather's been out of sorts,
But now we're homeward bound, for certain we'll rest and …
      do it all o'r again for,
Tis a sailor's life for me, ohhh off to the high ole sea!

Kittye Williams
©2008

A Pirate's Life for Me
(Being a Pirate at a Renaissance Faire)

Gather around ye tars and gobs,
We'll talk of faires from sea to sea,
You can sell wieners and you can sell nuts,
But it's a pirate's life for me!

When you go to the fair, everyone's there,
From knights to foot infantry.
There are fairies and imps and nobles and rogues,
But it's a pirate's life for me!

Some people go and cheer the joust,
Others the wenches to see,
But I'd rather swagger from tavern to pub,
It's a pirate's life for me!

Sweat out yer day in yer hoops and yer skirts,
Prance around in yer noble finery,
But give me a tricorn', boots and slops,
It's a pirate's life for me!

I have no problem with you wearing a sword,
Unless it's bigger than thee,
But give me a cutlass and me old leather belt,
It's a pirate's life for me!

Nobles and lords have a standard to keep,
And must drink in their own company,
But a pirate can drink with the high and the low:
It's a pirate life for me!

Don't get us wrong; this is only a song,
And we don't mean to offend thee.
But just like we told you, a thousand times over,
It's a pirate's life for me!

Melody Sanders
©2008

Gabrielle, the Belle of the Ball

She was Gabrielle the Belle of The Pirate Ball.
The word had spread to every port o' call
That a beautiful lass who was known by all,
Was coming to the dance at the Marriott hall.
Gabrielle, The Belle of The Pirate Ball.

She'd been in the parade, on a float so tall,
In a gorgeous dress, not bought at the mall.
The mateys when they saw her, on their knees did fall.
Gabrielle The Belle of The Pirate Ball.

When she entered the party as many would recall,
The line to dance with her went to the far wall.
Her beauty even caused the band's tempo to stall.
Gabrielle the Belle of The Pirate Ball.

All the other women began to resign,
That their dresses didn't rate to her lovely design.
Each seemed like a meager little shawl
Compared to Gabrielle The Belle of The Pirate Ball.

Michael Muller
©2008

72

Prize Island

We were sailing in the northern latitudes,
A day off the Florida coast,
Water we had, and limes and bread,
It was a prize that we needed the most.

The crew had come aboard at Holetown,[1]
A fine bunch of salts if ye ask me,
But a man signs articles for treasure.
It's the reason we all put to sea.

The war with France had lingered
And Spain had come into the fight.
With so many enemies to choose from,
There was still nary a foe in sight.

The men were restless and weary,
But I feared no mutiny from below
For these were good English sailors
Men from Cardiff, and Portsmouth, and Wicklow.

A captain has to keep his reputation
By making sure he finds gold for his men.
A captain that can't find prizes
Will never get a crew again.

I was on deck talking to me helmsman,
A good lad from near Aberdeen,
When the lookout shouted down a sightin'
And it was the prettiest sight I'd ever seen.

---

[1] "Holetown" was one of the earliest English settlements in the Caribbean; it grew from a landing spot on Barbados and was named for "The Hole", the stream which provided a safe landing for settlers.

Me spyglass caught a sail on the horizon
And I ordered on more canvas for speed.
We had the weather gauge in our favor;
We'd have all of the wind we would need.

We soon gained ground on our quarry,
We'd be on her before the morning was out,
And with the crews that were manning me cannon
The outcome was never in doubt.

As we came within safe hailing distance
I caught a stench that I can still smell:
The ship was a filthy French slaver,
Carrying poor damned souls straight to Hell.

Me men realized it was a slaver
And the ship went as silent as the grave;
In me crew were many a Redleg[2]
And even a runaway slave.

I called down from the quarterdeck
But me crew had already stood to.
This was a decision for all of us
And I asked them what they wanted to do.

"Men, we'll find no gold here,
Not till they've sold off their slaves.
We'd be fightin' to free men from bondage
And for that I won't wager your graves."

74

---

[2] "Redlegs" were white slaves or indentured servants in the New World.

"This is a decision for all of us,
One we must make to a man.
Do we sail away from the danger?
Or do we do what little good we can?"

The cheer with which the crew answered
Must have caused the French to turn white
'Cause they loosed their sails and their colors
And gave up to us without a fight.

My men seemed a trifle disappointed,
Especially the ex-slave Shombay.[3]
We all wanted to do a little cutting
But we'd save it for some other day.

I'll never forget crossing onto that vessel:
The smells, the sounds, the blood.
So many of the poor wretches were dying
But we did whatever we could.

We freed near two hundred that morning,
Many women, some children, but mostly men.
Some stood on the deck in silence,
Others shed tears to be free again.

But some danced wild savage dances
And called out to their gods in the sky,
Those white smiles in those inky black faces
I'll remember till the day I die.

75

---

[3] "Shombay is Swahili and translates "He who walks like a lion."

Both ships got underway before nightfall
And we sailed south-southeast all next day,
Till we spotted an island off of Cuba
A proper place for these people to stay.

It had fresh water, wild pigs and some coconuts
And not another soul that we could see;
If our friends were going to survive here
The world would have to let them be.

The Frenchies we left on the island
After making them bury the slaves who had died
And I can't think of a more proper memorial
Than the tears the big Shombay cried.

What happened, you ask, to the French slavers?
Well, your guess is as good as mine,
But I may find out more in the future:
I mean to visit that place again sometime.

After three days we left the island,
Without gold or anything we could spend,
But there wasn't a single member of me "bloodthirsty" crew
Who didn't feel like we were richer men.

Stephen Sanders
©2008

"Pirate's First Mate"
By Kenneth King, ©2008

A Galley Cook's Lament

Upon a barren ledge of rock,
Sat a man in a state of shock.
His beady black eyes surveyed the spit of land,
As the rustling palm trees swayed on the strand.

He fingered the knife in his belt,
It was cold as ice that he felt.
It was a mistake, now he knew,
To let the men begin to chew.

Salamungundie was more than the normal fare,
A stew of things, a few carrots, potatoes cut in squares.
He'd added the onions, the rice and the meats,
But it was the weevils from the hardtack
                that were special treats.

The Captain had bellowed a gigantic roar,
One that could be heard for miles or more,
"Bring me that cook!" he spit out the stew upon the plate,
"What is the meaning of these weevils I ate?"

The poor pirate looked down at the floor,
And wondered how close it was to the door?
"'Twas just a wee bit o' protein I added for taste,
They are quite dead!" the cook said in haste.

But it was far too late for the Captain of Fate,
"You tried to poison me you filthy ingrate!
For that you'll be marooned on a spit of land,
With this stew that is something less than grand."

So there he sat and pondered the pot of goo
And some passing flies dove into the stew.
He took his knife and stirred them in,
And tasted the food of bugs within.

"Why, this was pretty good," he thought,
"Some flies and weevils in the pot,
"How could it be bad," he thought as he ate,
"If nothing else it will make good fish bait."

Shari Land
©2008

The Hellion Betrayed

I sit alone beside m' fire,
My life and times to revisit.
The days of rollick and of ire,
They are all my lovers.

The roar of the cannon,
The fire, the flame;
The smoke that billows aloft
The deck quaking 'neath the feet.

The riches, the drink, the men all a' plenty,
The dances, of them, I had me a many.
The dice, the cards, the games o' chance;
The oath, the dare, I took every risk.

The rig sighing in the breeze,
The deck, weathered and worn.
The sails crisply snapping,
All were a song, sung only to me.

The sighting, the chase;
The blood set ablaze.
The prize set a'fore me,
Twas within m' gaze.

The lootings, the takings,
The sinking of ships.
Of these things, I was so great,
None could stand 'gainst me.

For sure and for certain
I commanded and was obeyed;
For none would gainsay me
And none would fail.

Until that cursed day,
Day most befouled;
When into my path;
A liar didst befall me.

With words oh so sweet,
Words of entreaty did speak.
With hope my heart did beat,
And in turn, my knees did grow weak.

Ah, but golden words soon turn,
Sweetness nay more, only slag.
He turned 'gainst me, left me to burn
Saying "I care not for this slattern hag."

From me they took all my silver and gold,
My ships and my men, my freedom … my spirit.
For a few pounds, my life had been sold;
Scorned and laughed at, ever will I hear it.

For punishment, I was not hanged.
No prison for me nor tied to the Wapping stick;
Nay, for a woman out of her place I was declaimed;
Left to rot upon land, for all my days … such a cruel trick.

So now I sit alone beside m' fire,
My life and times to revisit.
The days of rollick and of ire,
They were once my lovers.

Kittye Williams
©2008

The Old Sea Captain

As I pulled my carriage
To the veranda stairs
He was standing tall
With a mournful air
I climbed the stairs
And hid my fear
Of the Old Sea Captain
Coming near.
His eyes did soften
And his face did smile
Pushing away my fear
For a little while
"Would you like a room
For the night, Kind Sir?
There's a storm brewin' up
It should cause quite a stir."
He shook his head
And said, thanks, but no
He couldn't stay long
He would soon have to go
He was shipping out soon
Into stormy waters
But just wanted a last look
At what really mattered.
"I used to stay here
Long ago
Watch the waves toss
And feel the wind blow
Wonder if I could take a look
At the old room I shared
With the one woman I loved
With the one woman who cared."

I could tell he'd been at sea
For a very long time
His oilskin coat and boots
Had the smell of brine
The lines in his face
Were like maps on paper
His long strong fingers
Looked waxy like tapers
I said, "Be my guest
There's but a few here now.
Storm scares them from travelin'
Very far anyhow."
I let him in my inn that sits
On a cliff over looking the sea
He had an odd reaction
When my small daughter ran to me.
He looked sad
As he looked into her face
"She reminds me of my own little girl"
As a tear began to trace
A path of longing down to his
Whiskered jaw
"Haven't seen my baby girl
In quite a while."
He asked if my mother lived here still
Her raven hair would catch the wind
He'd always thought she was the most
Beautiful woman in the end
I told him that her raven hair
Had turned to silver by the time
The angels came to take her to Heaven
To ease her broken heart and make her sad face shine.
He looked at me with sad eyes

His tears seeming to run a race
"I should have been there to hold
Her hand and cup her face
But I was lost, Lost to myself
And lost to the world
Sailin' fer Davy Jones
In a sea of swirl
Just thought I'd check on my favorite girls
Before I have to go
Did some things I shouldn't have
Just thought that you should know
Ol' Davy Jones is a harsh taskmaster
Down beneath the sea
I snuck away for a short time
But he'll be looking for me."
I felt a tear begin to fall
Across my cheek and face.
Thought I could see a resemblance
In the mirror I could trace
"Papa?" I asked with a lump in my throat
"Is it you have come back to me?
Momma said your ship sank
To the bottom of the sea."
"I have, but only briefly
To remind me why I strive
To mend my ways and remember the days
When last I was alive
So pray for me child, Davy Jones will listen
Pray hard, and often, and long
Pray I escape my watery doom
To hear the angels song."
Then he hugged me and kissed me
With a father's strong caring.
And seemed to vanish to nothingness

While I stood there staring
And the lightning flashed and the thunder rolled
As the waves crashed on the shore
The wind blew and the storm surged
And I knew I'd see my father no more.
Just an Old Sea Captain
But no - so much more
Death could not contain him
And he came to my front door
And now I pray every night
Pray his ways to mend
So he can get to Heaven
To be with my mother again.

Pamala A. Williams
©2007

One day in the life...

The smell of the ocean is mighty fine when standing on a deck.
The wood, the sails, the pitch and all, together make the wreck
She's not much to look upon but she's all a crew can need
To sail the seas of liberty from the King's bloody bead.

The sun beats down upon our faces, the winds blow hard and fast
The sails unfurled, the ropes all curled, the boson climbs a mast.
A cabin boy walks true to port, and gathers bucket and brush
Every day of freedom on this ship makes life more than a rush

Night falls hard, the winds die down, and rations are passed around
The men sing tales of battles won, and treasures that abound
Then spies the lookout's watchful eye a port and starboard lamp:
"Avast!" he cries! "A ship is come, and they see us for a ramp"!

The captain shouts his men to arms, "Way anchor, prepare for boarding!
Strike the colors, gunners prepare, we'll get some spoils for hoarding!"
Cannons fire, wood shivers and cracks, as the battle rages through
Blood, sweat and tears stain the deck but men keep fighting true

The sun rises on the floating hulks, bodies strewn from stem to bow
Men wander wounded here and there, some stunned, some asking "how?"
The English lost again that day, and pirates won their treasure.
Best join this group of privateers, their focus beyond measure!

No quarter is given otherwise aboard the good ship *Carter*
No life to save, save you and yours, nothing left to barter
We sail forever with this crew, a life of discipline and wonder
Our freedom won, new life begun, our futures yet to ponder.

The smell of the ocean is mighty fine when standing on a deck.
The wood, the sails, the pitch and all, together make the wreck
She's not much to look upon but she's all a crew can need
To sail the seas of liberty from the King's bloody bead.

Sandra L. Harris
©2008

Raising the Black Flag

Golden flames, purple and pink:
The colors of the sunset
Blend and flow among the clouds
As we take in our lines
And slip away from the dock.
And the crew counts the dolphins
As we escape down the channel to the sea.

Home falls away behind us
As we close with the perils
Of a life spent in the sweet trade:
Bad food, worse water, eels in the rigging,
French muskets, Spanish cannon, Dutch rope,
Dying of thirst becalmed in the doldrums
Or drowning when the ship comes apart in a gale.

We measure these dangers against
Phantom coins in untaken treasure chests
Spent on red wine nights in exotic ports
With companions paid to make us feel like gods.
They do their jobs well.
And when we sail we have the wind in our hair
And the horizon to scan for prizes.

A pirate's life is most likely short,
A pirate's death is most likely sharp.
But we are not slaves to any wage
And we call no man "sire" or "squire."
In the end, it's not the gold that sets our sails;
'Tis freedom and the fair expectation of a better life
That raises our black flags.

Stephen Sanders
©2008

The Siren of Superior

Freshwater mermaid
Siren of Superior
Warming herself
This autumn day
On the black rock.
Her flowing hair glistens
in the forbidden sunshine.
A keen-eyed sailor
On a passing schooner
Sees a shape against the cliff
Reaching for his spyglass
He sees only a splash of wave
On the black rock
In the shallows
And a glistening fish
That disappears
Into the icy depths.

Debra Estes Petersen
©2008

The Voyage Begins

The tides have come in, the sails are run out
We's rounding the point to the wide open sea
The captain says "full sail, all ahead south!"
To capture the tradewinds and see what may be . . .

"South to the lanes, what prizes await!
So run out the guns boys, the treasure's at hand
We're light on provisions, but heavy on fate
No quarter be given if they make a fool's stand!"

A sail ahead, yes? Too early to tell
More sail to give chase we will take the prize
When death comes to call you will hear the bell
As you go to sleep with pennies for eyes

The captain roars "faster!" we stand to the rails
And hungrily dream of the decks awash red
A dark howling rises as we make full sails
And dark clouds gather directly ahead . . .

Chuck Burrows
©2008

To be continued . . .

Coming soon:

Another anthology of pirate works from the crew of the Adventure! Planned for the winter of 2009, this voyage will include more poems, short stories, and new original artwork. If you would like to be a part of the crew for this next great voyage, email Blackbead, Master of the Adventure at Blackbeads_tc@yahoo.com!
A share of the plunder goes to all hands worthy of their salt!

www.ingramcontent.com/pod-product-compliance
Lightning Source LLC
Chambersburg PA
CBHW081236090426
42738CB00016B/3320